BREAKING BREAD

GROUP STUDIES

LEADER'S GUIDE

Edited by
ANDREW ROBERTS

The Bible Reading Fellowship
15 The Chambers, Vineyard
Abingdon OX14 3FE
brf.org.uk

The Bible Reading Fellowship (BRF) is a Registered Charity (233280)

ISBN 978 0 85746 858 1
First published 2020
10 9 8 7 6 5 4 3 2 1 0
All rights reserved

Acknowledgements

Scripture quotations marked NRSV are taken from The New Revised Standard Version
of the Bible, Anglicised edition, copyright © 1989, 1995 by the Division of Christian
Education of the National Council of the Churches of Christ in the United States of
America. Used by permission. All rights reserved.

Scripture quotations marked NIV are taken from The Holy Bible, New International
Version (Anglicised edition) copyright © 1979, 1984, 2011 by Biblica. Used by
permission of Hodder & Stoughton Publishers, a Hachette UK company. All rights
reserved. 'NIV' is a registered trademark of Biblica. UK trademark number 1448790.

Every effort has been made to trace and contact copyright owners for material used
in this resource. We apologise for any inadvertent omissions or errors, and would
ask those concerned to contact us so that full acknowledgement can be made in
the future.

A catalogue record for this book is available from the British Library

Printed and bound in the UK by Zenith Media NP4 0DQ

Contents

About the writers

Rob Glenny is rector of the Radley, Sunningwell and Kennington benefice, situated between Oxford and Abingdon. Prior to ordination he read for degrees in theology at the universities of St Andrews and Oxford.

Derek Tidball was formerly the principal of London School of Theology. He is a prolific writer and a speaker in demand around the world. He is the New Testament editor for BRF's 'Really Useful Guides' series.

Naomi Starkey is a curate in the Church in Wales, working in Welsh and English across six rural churches on the Llyn Peninsula. She previously worked as a BRF commissioning editor from 1997 to 2015 and has written a number of books, including *The Recovery of Joy* (BRF, 2017) and *The Recovery of Hope* (BRF, 2016).

Liz Kent is director of Wesley Study Centre, Durham University, and minister for Chester le Street, Birtley and Pelton Methodist Churches. She studied law at Liverpool University prior to training for Methodist ministry. She is interested in questions of holiness, Christian ethics and mission, and completed PhD research at Durham University exploring the church and eating disorders. She is a keen drummer, footballer and outdoor pursuits enthusiast. She is married to Ian, also a Methodist minister, and they have two daughters.

Introduction

> They devoted themselves to the apostles' teaching and fellowship, to the breaking of bread and the prayers. Awe came upon everyone, because many wonders and signs were being done by the apostles. All who believed were together and had all things in common; they would sell their possessions and goods and distribute the proceeds to all, as any had need. Day by day, as they spent much time together in the temple, they broke bread at home and ate their food with glad and generous hearts, praising God and having the goodwill of all the people. And day by day the Lord added to their number those who were being saved.
>
> ACTS 2:42–47 (NRSV)

Holy Habits is a way of life to be lived by disciples of Jesus individually and collectively. As Alison Morgan points out in the subtitle of her book *Following Jesus*, the plural of disciple is church. When Jesus calls us to follow, he gifts us others to journey with us, just as he gifted his first disciples – others who will help to teach us and who will learn from us; others who will pray with us and check how we are; others who will watch over us in love and keep us accountable in our discipleship. In the light of this, these Group Studies and the complementary daily Bible Reflections have been written for both group and personal usage. In this booklet, you will find material to help you as a church or a small group reflect together on the particular holy habit being explored.

The authors (who also wrote the complementary Holy Habits Bible Reflections; see page 62) have formed questions for reflection and discussion. Each author has selected two of the readings from the ten they wrote about and provided six questions on each for discussion. Some have a more personal focus, while others relate more to the church or group as whole. With questions of a more personal nature, you may wish to invite people to discuss these in the confidence of pairs and then make time for anyone to share a response with the whole group if they would like to. This approach can also be a good way of making sure everyone has a chance to share if your group has newcomers or people who are shy or dominant.

You will then find a series of take-home questions about the habit. These have been collated from questions submitted by the authors, which mean they vary in style, tone and focus. As such, you may find some more helpful than others, so feel free to add or amend questions. As you work together, you might like to see what emerges in the responses and see if some of the questions should be revisited regularly (perhaps annually or every six months) as a way of reviewing the life of your small group or church as a discipleship community against the picture Luke offers us in Acts 2. Similarly, individuals could be invited to keep a journal to regularly reflect on their living of the holy habits.

In Acts 2:47, Luke says the believers enjoyed 'the goodwill of all the people', so there are also some creative ideas for ways in which your church or group could collectively practise the habit being explored in the local or wider community. These are thought-starter ideas, so be open to other ideas that emerge in your conversations.

You will also find some prayers and creative media ideas for this habit at the back of the book.

In all of this, keep your hearts and minds open to the Holy Spirit and be alert to the wonders of God's grace and the signs of God's love that emerge as, individually and collectively, you live this down-to-earth, holy way of life that Luke invites us to imitate.

Session outline

One way your group time could be structured:

- **Opening prayer**
  (for example, the Holy Habits prayer on page 59)

- **Music moment**
  (see 'Listen', page 61)

- **Bible reading**

- **Reflection**

- **Discussion questions**

- Time for stories, testimonies or questions/issues that arise from the discussion

- Prayer

- **Ideas to do as a group**
  Spend a few minutes to agree when this will be carried out or to come up with other ideas

- **Take-home questions/creative media ideas**

- Closing prayer

| Rob Glenny

Week 1

The power of hospitality

Read Genesis 18:1–6

The Lord appeared to Abraham by the oaks of Mamre, as he sat at the entrance of his tent in the heat of the day. He looked up and saw three men standing near him. When he saw them, he ran from the tent entrance to meet them, and bowed down to the ground. He said, 'My lord, if I find favour with you, do not pass by your servant. Let a little water be brought, and wash your feet, and rest yourselves under the tree. Let me bring a little bread, that you may refresh yourselves, and after that you may pass on – since you have come to your servant.' So they said, 'Do as you have said.' And Abraham hastened into the tent to Sarah, and said, 'Make ready quickly three measures of choice flour, knead it, and make cakes.'   (NRSV)

Reflection

In 2017, as right-wing protesters marched through the city of Birmingham, a mosque in the centre of the city responded by throwing open its doors for the afternoon and hosting a tea party. The place of worship was bedecked in Union flags and bunting, while inside Muslims served their community with tea, coffee and cakes. Everyone was invited to attend and to share conversation with their neighbours, as well as discover a little more about the people who, on the other side of the city, were being demonised.

We may be familiar with Abraham's encounter with these three figures as a picture of hospitality. But what is striking about the detail in this passage is that, like Birmingham Central Mosque, this is a holistic hospitality on offer. Abraham goes the extra mile. Rather than waiting for the three men to find him, instead he runs through the heat of the day away from his tent to meet them. Rather than greeting them as equals, he bows to the ground in humility and service. Rather than simply offering sustenance, Abraham invites the strangers to wash, rest, eat and drink. Rather than giving ordinary food, Abraham gives instruction to provide the best of what he and Sarah have to offer.

The hospitality of a shared meal provides an opportunity to do more than simply eat. A community that breaks bread together, or one which offers radical hospitality to strangers, is providing an opportunity for both holistic refreshment and meaningful encounter.

> Embracing God, meet us in friend and stranger and help our whole being find its rest in you. Amen

Questions

1 What does the appearance of strangers tell you about how we see God's face in others?

2 Where, in your local context, might you need to venture to spend time with those with whom you are unfamiliar?

3 What does 'going the extra mile' to offer hospitality look like in your community?

4 'After that you may pass on.' How can you equip those who gather with you to continue their journey with God when they leave?

5 Abraham and Sarah's act of hospitality prepares them to welcome new life into their family. What do you need to do to prepare yourself for welcoming new life or new people into the family of the church?

6 How might you break bread to welcome or befriend others or commission others as they journey on?

• • •

Week 1

Idea to do as a group

> **1** Hold a meal as a community and invite people round whom you don't know very well. Think about the ways in which you can offer holistic hospitality, as well as simply feeding people. How could a simple act of breaking bread be part of this?

Take-home questions

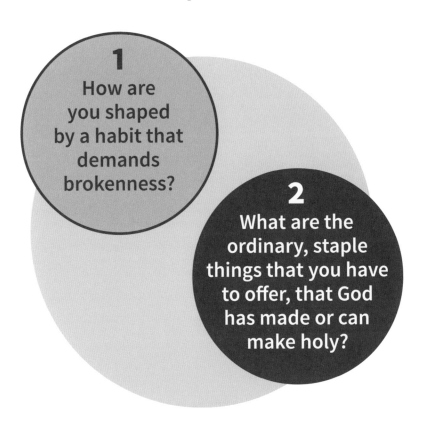

1
How are you shaped by a habit that demands brokenness?

2
What are the ordinary, staple things that you have to offer, that God has made or can make holy?

| Rob Glenny

Week 2

The splendour of heaven touching earth

Read Exodus 25:23–30

You shall make a table of acacia wood, two cubits long, one cubit wide, and a cubit and a half high. You shall overlay it with pure gold, and make a moulding of gold round it. You shall make round it a rim a handbreadth wide, and a moulding of gold round the rim. You shall make for it four rings of gold, and fasten the rings to the four corners at its four legs. The rings that hold the poles used for carrying the table shall be close to the rim. You shall make the poles of acacia wood, and overlay them with gold, and the table shall be carried with these. You shall make its plates and dishes for incense, and its flagons and bowls with which to pour drink-offerings; you shall make them of pure gold. And you shall set the bread of the Presence on the table before me always.   (NRSV)

Reflection

The construction of the temple is one of the key events to take place in the second half of Exodus. As is made clear by the sheer volume of gold that is required to construct the table for the bread of the Presence, this is a piece of architecture which has a purpose beyond being simply functional. It was there to convey something that words fall short of describing: the glory of God. The bread itself has a delightful ambiguity in translation, one which can be read in a variety of eucharistic understandings: it means either the bread that *is* the presence of God or the bread that is *in* the presence of God. We don't know for certain.

Both Jews and Christians share a pattern of ritualised breaking of bread, sometimes in surroundings intended to convey God's majestic glory, sometimes in far more humble settings. What matters is not the objects or furnishings in themselves, but what they point us towards. These are moments when we are invited to draw near to the glory of God, to catch a glimpse of the heavenly reality breaking into our own. Like the table in the temple, or the temple itself, this moment of encounter should clothe us as those who are covered and filled with that glory.

> God of glory, break through our dull vision and show us the splendour of heaven touching earth. Amen

Questions

1 How does the architecture at your place of worship draw you closer to God? In particular, in what ways does it help with the breaking of bread? Would any changes to the layout of the building be helpful?

2 Paul writes that we are 'God's temple' (1 Corinthians 3:16). What about you points to the glory of God?

3 The Celts referred to 'thin places', where heaven and earth feel particularly close. Where might one of these places be for you? Is this a place where you break bread? Could it be?

4 What parts of your life feel merely functional? How could you alter your perception to see them as glory-filled?

5 What do you think the relationship is between beauty and mission?

6 'And you shall set the bread of the Presence on the table before me always.' What are your permanent reminders of God's provision and presence?

• • •

Week 2

Idea to do as a group

> **1** Find some large stones and, with paint or pens, decorate them with pictures or words of scripture. Place these around your community as symbols of God's glory breaking into the ordinary parts of our lives. If possible, invite a local school or other groups to go searching for them in the surrounding area.

Take-home question

1
When you break bread together, who is absent from the gathering, and why? How could these people be invited to experience the blessing of breaking bread?

| Derek Tidball

Week 3

God's environmental policy

Read Psalm 104:10–14

He makes springs pour water into the ravines; it flows between the mountains. They give water to all the beasts of the field; the wild donkeys quench their thirst. The birds of the sky nest by the waters; they sing among the branches. He waters the mountains from his upper chambers; the land is satisfied by the fruit of his work. He makes grass grow for the cattle, and plants for people to cultivate – bringing forth food from the earth. (NIV)

Reflection

We are increasingly concerned about global warming and what we are doing to the environment, and rightly so. Yet there is a more fundamental truth about the environment which saves us from fear while encouraging us to act responsibly. It's not our environmental policy – it's God's.

When God created the earth, he made it to function in a certain sustainable way. Springs deep in the earth and rain from high in the sky provide the necessary water to irrigate crops and plants. Provision is made for all living creatures. The psalmist also rejoices that creation is more than merely functional – it is also bountiful. Birds sing songs of praise and, in the verse that follows our reading, it is said that wine 'gladdens human hearts'.

Planet earth is richly resourced. Our responsibility is to manage it properly and to share its produce with those in need. God has ensured that we have enough for all our needs, if not for our greed. How absurd that one-third of the world goes hungry daily, while another third suffer from over-eating. Far from encouraging self-satisfied enjoyment and over-indulgence, the words of this psalm encourage us to fall in line with God's design and intention for all of his creation and his creatures.

> Generous God, whenever I break bread, may I rejoice in your generous provision for my needs and learn from you how to share with those who are hungry. Help us to manage your creation with care. Amen

Questions

1 What characteristics would you attribute to God as the creator of the earth?

2 How do you square the picture in Psalm 104 of God's bounty with the poverty and hunger we see in our world today?

3 What attitude should Christians adopt to global warming and the environmental crisis?

4 How can bread be broken in ways that both celebrate the goodness of God in creation and identify with those who have little or no bread?

5 There are traditionally four acts associated with services of Holy Communion: thanksgiving, blessing, breaking and sharing. How might these acts shape your attitudes and behaviours with regard to the care of creation?

6 What significance do you give to God's plan for 'a new heaven and a *new earth*' (see 2 Peter 3:13 and Revelation 21:1–5)? And how might the act of breaking bread be an anticipation of this (Matthew 26:26–29)?

• • •

Week 3

Idea to do as a group

1 If you have a missional activity that involves eating together, simply break and share some bread at the beginning of the meal and give thanks for the presence of the Lord Jesus at the meal table. To be fully hospitable, make sure the bread is gluten- and dairy-free.

Take-home questions

1

How can breaking bread 'day by day' (to use Luke's phrase in Acts 2:47) help you to be mindful of and thankful for God's provision of food and other good gifts?

2

How might breaking bread help you to be mindful of and responsive to those who are hungry in our world?

| Derek Tidball

Week 4

Life-giving bread

Read Isaiah 55:1–2

'Come, all you who are thirsty, come to the waters; and you who have no money, come, buy and eat! Come, buy wine and milk without money and without cost. Why spend money on what is not bread, and your labour on what does not satisfy? Listen, listen to me, and eat what is good, and you will delight in the richest of fare.'

(NIV)

Reflection

Within a mile of my home there are five major supermarkets. Their shelves groan and their offers all cry out, 'Buy me, buy me!' Consequently, it's hard to identify with the pictures of hardship we sometimes see on the news when people in famine-stricken areas scramble over each other to get a bowl of rice or some bottles of water from a relief agency. Yet, that's more like the situation Isaiah addresses. Middle Eastern lands were often parched and struggled with very poor harvests. There was a desperate need to quench people's thirst and fill their empty stomachs with life-giving bread. But how?

Through Isaiah, God paints a picture of the spiritual desolation Israel has suffered in the exile, but he promises them that a new day of grace is dawning, when he will freely remedy their ills and rebuild their nation. The remedy is not without cost, but he will foot the bill himself, rather than charge it to them.

Three things are necessary for it to happen. One: as with any invitation, they need to accept it. Two: they need to put all their store on this invitation and not look to other solutions, whether political or religious. These may look attractive but will prove a false economy, wasting their merger resources. Three: responding involves listening, not only to God's invitation but also to all his other wisdom and instructions, so that they might begin to live again.

Jesus updated the invitation: 'I am the bread of life. Whoever comes to me will never go hungry, and whoever believes in me will never be thirsty' (John 6:35). He awaits our RSVP.

> Lord, teach me to listen to you and feed on you, the bread of life. Amen

Questions

1 In what ways are contemporary men and women thirsty?

2 The invitation is addressed to those who 'have no money'. To what extent is one of the problems of the western contemporary church that it is too rich and not poverty-stricken before God? Does Revelation 3:14–22 apply to you?

3 Read the beatitudes in Matthew 5:3–10. How do they provide a commentary on these verses from Isaiah?

4 Give examples of how you expend energy and hard-earned money 'on what does not satisfy'.

5 Isaiah warns about spending money on what is not bread. Jesus said, 'I am the bread of life' (John 6:35), but what did he mean by this?

6 How can you practise the holy habit of breaking bread at home (as the believers did in Acts 2:46) as one way of delighting in the riches of God's grace?

• • •

Week 4

Ideas to do as a group

1 Offer bread-making sessions to others e.g. local children or if possible those who are served by the local foodbank. At the end of the baking, break some bread together and give thanks for God's blessings.

2 If you are considering a fresh expression of church in your area, have a look at some of the bread-making churches – e.g. Somewhere Else in Liverpool (**somewhere-else.org.uk**) or the House of Bread (**facebook.com/h.o.b.stafford**) – and prayerfully consider if this might be a model you are being called to adopt.

Take-home question

1

In many of these passages, bread is mentioned alongside other food and drink. How do/could the holy habits of breaking bread and eating together relate?

| Naomi Starkey

Week 5

Praying like Jesus

Read Luke 11:1–4

One day Jesus was praying in a certain place. When he finished, one of his disciples said to him, 'Lord, teach us to pray, just as John taught his disciples.' He said to them, 'When you pray, say: "Father, hallowed be your name, your kingdom come. Give us each day our daily bread. Forgive us our sins, for we also forgive everyone who sins against us. And lead us not into temptation."' (NIV)

Reflection

The words of this prayer are so familiar – and so often introduced with words to the effect of 'Let us pray as Jesus himself taught us' – that we can overlook the wonder of it. This is the Son of God teaching his followers how to pray to his Father. These are the kind of things we should say to God himself, and, as we do so, we are following the example of Jesus.

Praise comes before petition, reminding us whom we are addressing: not a generalised higher power or anonymous god, but the one we know as Father. And it is Father whom we ask for daily bread, echoing Jesus' teaching in Matthew 7 and Luke 11, where he tells his listeners how the Father delights to supply their needs, more so than any earthly father.

Apparently the phrase about daily bread should be translated as, 'Carry on giving us our bread each day', and the bread here is usually understood as daily needs and what we need to keep us going, rather than a specific loaf of bread. Jewish thought didn't divide the world into physical and spiritual in the way we tend to, however, and we do well to remember that we can ask God to supply whatever we need to keep us going each day, whether a loaf of bread or a dose of courage.

Having the Eucharist at the heart of our regular worship is an essential reminder that ours is an embodied faith. We don't just think about the sacrifice of Christ's body; we eat and drink it. Doing so, we ask the Father, though his Spirit, to feed us so that we are strong enough to resist temptation, to forgive others and to bear daily witness to his grace.

> Lord, teach me to pray.

Questions

1 Which is your favourite phrase in the Lord's Prayer, and why?

2 Which phrase do you find hardest to pray, and why?

3 How might praying for 'daily bread' connect with being spiritually fed by the Eucharist?

4 In what other ways might praying for daily bread connect with our lives and the lives of those with whom and for whom we pray?

5 How important do you find prayer in preparing to receive the Eucharist?

6 How important do you think it is to say the Lord's Prayer as part of the Eucharist?

• • •

Week 5

Idea to do as a group

1 As a group, visit a local church with a very different worship tradition to your own and take part in the Eucharist. Reflect together afterwards on what you did and didn't find helpful in terms of drawing you closer to God.

Take-home question

1

Reflect on how and when the Eucharist is celebrated in your local church. Is it at the heart of worship – or does it feel like a bit of an afterthought?

| Naomi Starkey

Week 6

Don't just look – touch!

Read Luke 24:36b–39, 41–43

Jesus himself stood among [the disciples] and said to them, 'Peace be with you.' They were startled and frightened, thinking they saw a ghost. He said to them, 'Why are you troubled, and why do doubts rise in your minds? Look at my hands and my feet. It is I myself! Touch me and see; a ghost does not have flesh and bones, as you see I have'... And while they still did not believe it because of joy and amazement, he asked them, 'Do you have anything here to eat?' They gave him a piece of broiled fish, and he took it and ate it in their presence. (NIV)

Week 6

Reflection

Throughout these post-resurrection encounters, Jesus is preparing his followers for their work of going out and sharing the good news. It is consoling to see in this episode how he urges them to overcome their doubts and connect with him physically – look at him, touch him, watch him eat fish. He is no ghost, nor simply resuscitated, but made gloriously alive, while still scarred by his suffering. Even when the disciples' fear and doubt have turned to 'joy and amazement', they continue to struggle to grasp what is happening – and who is standing before them.

This episode is a counterbalance to Thomas' experience (John 20:24–29), when Jesus comments, 'Blessed are those who have not seen and yet have believed.' We can be tempted to hear that as 'Pathetic are those who lack really strong faith', but here we see there's no shame in wanting some kind of physical reassurance to build up our hesitant faith.

'Growing in faith' is sometimes felt to be a matter of simply cultivating a strong inner certainty – but the Eucharist provides a vital reminder that faith is also about seeing, touching, tasting and receiving what God wants to give us, literally as well as spiritually. Faith is also about living out what we believe in acts of witness to an indifferent world – caring for the needy, the lonely, the marginalised. We believe in an incarnate God; we need to model an incarnate faith too.

> In what ways could your church do more to model incarnate faith to the surrounding community?

Questions

1 How do you think the Eucharist can help convey God's presence to those who find it hard to believe in what they cannot test with their senses?

2 Has the Eucharist helped you admit – or process – doubts and worries about your faith? If so, how?

3 What is the significance of Jesus asking for fish to eat?

4 What comfort might the Eucharist offer those who are mourning loved ones?

5 How important is Jesus' physical resurrection for your experience of the Eucharist?

6 If you met Jesus face-to-face, what would you say to him?

• • •

Idea to do as a group

> **1** With the help of your church leader, think about devising a Eucharist with a different feel to your usual celebration. How about an outdoor service, one in café church style, or even a jazz or goth Eucharist? (Look online for more information.)

Take-home questions

1
Do you think
the Eucharist
offers a 'way in' to
faith for seekers? How
might this work
in your church
context?

2
How
significant are
the Passover roots
of the Eucharist
for you?

| Liz Kent

Week 7

'Come and have breakfast'

Read John 21:8–13

The other disciples followed in the boat, towing the net full of fish, for they were not far from shore, about a hundred metres. When they landed, they saw a fire of burning coals there with fish on it, and some bread. Jesus said to them, 'Bring some of the fish you have just caught.' So Simon Peter climbed back into the boat and dragged the net ashore. It was full of large fish, 153, but even with so many the net was not torn. Jesus said to them, 'Come and have breakfast.' None of the disciples dared ask him, 'Who are you?' They knew it was the Lord. Jesus came, took the bread and gave it to them, and did the same with the fish.　(NIV)

Reflection

In this encounter, the risen Jesus goes to his disciples, who have returned to fishing after his death. On the beach, Jesus prepares breakfast and invites them to bring their own contribution of the fish they've just caught.

What is happening is astonishing. Only a little time before, Jesus had been crucified, and yet here he is, alive and present with them. At the same time, there is a sense of normality – fishing was what the disciples had done their whole lives. Bread and fish for breakfast was pretty normal, too. When Jesus takes the bread and gives it to them, they experience the resurrected Jesus present with them in the normality of a working day and an ordinary meal.

In the work canteen, Sarah always felt anxious and out of place. It was only when her colleague Jenny called to her 'come and have lunch with us' and offered her a seat at a table with two other colleagues that the fear began to subside. In the middle of an ordinary day, an extraordinary moment of invitation opened up a conversation over lunch which would change her life.

Where do you sense the presence of the risen Jesus in the ordinary meals you share with colleagues, friends or family?

> God of the extraordinary and the everyday, help me to remember as I break bread and eat 'ordinary' meals that you are present with me. As you invite me, help me invite others to meet you and encounter your love. Amen

Questions

1 Why do you think the disciples went fishing?

2 In the gospels, Jesus is often the guest at a meal in someone's home. On this occasion, he is the host. What difference do you think this makes?

3 When you eat together in Christian community, breaking bread together, what is the significance of everybody bringing some food to share if they're able?

4 Sometimes breaking bread will challenge us to meet people's basic needs before they are able to respond to Jesus. How have you seen this in your situation?

5 Are you ever worried about asking questions in a church/faith setting? Why? Might asking questions as you break bread or eat together help?

6 In our self-reliant, self-service world, do you think there is something significant about taking food and actually giving it to someone else?

• • •

Week 7

Idea to do as a group

> **1** Spend time with your small group or with another person making bread. As you make the bread, reflect on what you have learned about this holy habit. Talk and pray about who you will share the bread with when it is baked.

Take-home questions

1

What is your earliest memory of Communion/Lord's Supper/Eucharist? Can you recall what you felt or thought and any questions you had?

2

Can you think of an occasion where breaking bread (e.g. in the celebration of Communion or in a meal of Christian fellowship) has been a particularly significant moment in your faith journey?

| Liz Kent

Week 8

Eat, drink, remember

Read 1 Corinthians 11:23–26

For I received from the Lord what I also passed on to you: the Lord Jesus, on the night he was betrayed, took bread, and when he had given thanks, he broke it and said, 'This is my body, which is for you; do this in remembrance of me.' In the same way, after supper he took the cup, saying, 'This cup is the new covenant in my blood; do this, whenever you drink it, in remembrance of me.' For whenever you eat this bread and drink this cup, you proclaim the Lord's death until he comes. (NIV)

Reflection

This passage contains what has come to be recognised as the most succinct description of the practice of Communion in the early church.

Paul is clear with the Corinthians that what he is transmitting to them is the practice which he received. It contains the actions of thanksgiving, breaking bread, drinking wine and remembering. Together, these practices witness to what has taken place in Jesus' death and also look to the future hope of his promised return.

The emphasis on 'in remembrance' means that Communion liturgies are focused around retelling the story of God's saving love made visible in the life, death and resurrection of Jesus. In eating bread and drinking wine, we remember Jesus with thanksgiving. The beautiful simplicity of the act of breaking bread and sharing wine means it crosses language, national and cultural boundaries. Christians across the world may differ in many ways, but in the central act of sharing bread and wine we are drawn to the heart of our faith: remembering Jesus.

Micah grew up in Uganda but came to study in the UK. He had been involved in his church at home and searched for a church near his student flat. He went one Sunday and found the songs were different, the preaching style was unfamiliar to him, the people were friendly but reserved, the church notices were nothing like at home. It was only as the bread was broken, the wine poured and both were shared that he felt he was truly part of the body of Christ.

> Lord Jesus, thank you that through the mystery, you come to us in the simplicity of bread and wine. Help me remember you today. Amen

Questions

1 Read the passage through slowly three times. What part of this account of sharing bread and wine stands out for you?

2 Paul passes on the tradition he received. Who passed on the tradition of breaking bread to you, and who have you passed it on to?

3 When we break bread with others, we become vulnerable before one another. How does that make you feel?

4 When Jesus takes the bread, he gives thanks. Were you brought up to 'say grace' before meals? Do you/would you find this helpful as a reminder to be thankful for the food we have?

5 Could you develop a simple daily practice of breaking a piece of bread at home and giving thanks?

6 When we break bread and share wine, how much time do we spend looking back to remember Jesus' death and resurrection, and how much time looking forward to his return?

• • •

Idea to do as a group

1 Share a meal with your small group and look in the New Testament at the different meals Jesus shared with people. As you eat, think about what sort of meal would help your friends meet Jesus – indoor or outdoor? Spontaneous or planned? Formal or informal? How might you break bread within this in a way other than Communion?

Take-home question

1

'Some things only fulfil their true potential after they have been broken.' This is true for the bread we share. Do you agree with the statement? Apart from bread, can you think of other examples?

For your notes

For your notes

Prayers

The Holy Habits prayer

Endurance produces character, and character produces hope,
   and hope does not disappoint us…
Gracious and ever-loving God, we offer our lives to you.
Help us always to be open to your Spirit in our thoughts
   and feelings and actions.
Support us as we seek to learn more about those habits of
   the Christian life
which, as we practise them, will form in us the character
   of Jesus
by establishing us in the way of faith, hope and love.
Amen

Prayer of thanksgiving

Creative, caring God, we can only begin to imagine how, on
that night surrounded by fear, violence and betrayal, our
life-giving Jesus took the day's bread, thanked you for it, broke
it, gave it to his companions and said, 'Take, eat. This is my
body given for you. Do this to remember me.'

After supper, he took the cup, thanked you again and gave it
to all saying, 'This cup is the new covenant of my blood, shed
for you and for everyone for the forgiveness of sin. Do this to
remember me.'

We remember that Jesus gave his life for us and for the whole
world. We believe the story of the resurrection, and we long to
share Christ's life:

Christ has died. Christ is alive. Christ will come again.

Prayers

Prayer of blessing

God the Creator of life in countryside and city,
God the Giver of resurrection life,
God the Spirit of love and life,
God bless us, and through us may our homes, our city,
    our world
be blessed in the name of God, Father, Son and Spirit.
Amen

Creative media

Creative media ideas

Watch

Cast Away (12, 2000, 2h23m)

In *Cast Away*, the struggle to survive and the scarcity of food mean that, on the castaway's return to civilisation, the emotional significance of various things including food is very noticeable. At one stage, Tom Hanks appears to try to share food with an inanimate object. This film is useful for a discussion of symbolism and of attaching value to an item.

- This film illustrates the overlapping of the holy habits of Eating Together and Breaking Bread. Is there something sacramental about the castaway's desire to share food with an inanimate object?
- How does this challenge our understanding of breaking bread and its relationship to eating together?

Read

Imagining Abundance

Visit imaginingabundance.co.uk/the-prospect-of-a-feast/living-bread. html for a fantastic series of reflections and questions around the theme of living bread.

Listen

'Breaking Bread' by Paul Field

Whole-church resources

Individual copy £4.99

Holy Habits is an adventure in Christian discipleship. Inspired by Luke's model of church found in Acts 2:42–47, it identifies ten habits and encourages the development of a way of life formed by them. These resources are designed to help churches explore the habits creatively in a range of contexts and live them out in whole-life, intergenerational, missional discipleship.

MISSIONAL DISCIPLESHIP RESOURCES FOR CHURCHES

HOLYHABITS

Original design by morsebrowndesign.co.uk & penguinboy.net

These new additions to the Holy Habits resources have been developed to help churches and individuals explore the Holy Habits through prayerful engagement with the Bible and live them out in whole-life, missional discipleship.

Bible Reflections   Edited by Andrew Roberts | Individual copy £3.99

Each set of Bible reading notes contains eight weeks of devotional material. Four writers bring different perspectives on the habit in question through their reflections on passages drawn from across the Bible narrative.

Group Studies   Edited by Andrew Roberts | Individual copy £6.99

Each leader's guide contains eight sessions of Bible study material, providing off-the-peg material to help churches get started or continue with Holy Habits. Each session includes a Bible passage, reflections, group questions, community/outreach ideas, art and media links and a prayer.

Find out more at holyhabits.org.uk
and brfonline.org.uk/collections/holy-habits
Download a leaflet for your church leadership at
brfonline.org.uk/holyhabitsdownload

Praise for the original Holy Habits resources

'Here are some varied and rich resources to help further deepen our discipleship of Christ, encouraging and enabling us to adopt the life-transforming habits that make for following Jesus.'

Revd Dr Martyn Atkins, Team Leader & Superintendent Minister, Methodist Central Hall, Westminster

'The Holy Habits resources will help you, your church, your fellowship group, to engage in a journey of discovery about what it really means to be a disciple today. I know you will be encouraged, challenged and inspired as you read and work your way through… There is lots to study together and pray about, and that can only be good as our churches today seek to bring about the kingdom of God.'

Revd Loraine Mellor, President of the Methodist Conference 2017/18

'The Holy Habits resources help weave the spiritual through everyday life. They're a great tool that just get better with use. They help us grow in our desire to follow Jesus as their concern is formation not simply information.'

Olive Fleming Drane and John Drane

'The Holy Habits resources are an insightful and comprehensive manual for living in the way of Jesus in the 21st century: an imaginative, faithful and practical gift for the church that will sustain and invigorate our life and mission in a demanding world. The Holy Habits resources are potentially transformational for a church.'

Revd Ian Adams, Mission Spirituality Adviser for Church Mission Society

'To understand the disciplines of the Christian life without practising them habitually is like owning a fine collection of soap but never having a wash. The team behind Holy Habits knows this, which is why they have produced these excellent and practical resources. Use them, and by God's grace you will grow in holiness.'

Paul Bayes, Bishop of Liverpool